Love, Death, and Flowing Water

ABIQUIU PRESS

LOVE, DEATH,

and

FLOWING WATER

A CYCLE OF THE SEASONS
IN ABIQUIU, NEW MEXICO

⤳⤲

ORO LYNN BENSON

ABIQUIU PRESS

This work of poetry is licensed under the Creative Commons Attribution-ShareAlike 4.0 International License. To view a copy of this license, visit http://creativecommons.org/licenses/by-sa/4.0/ or send a letter to Creative Commons, PO Box 1866, Mountain View, CA 94042, USA.

Cover Photograph and photographs on pages 30, 31, 50,51 by Oro Lynn Benson

Photograhps on pages ii, iii, xii, 1, 16, 17, 70, 71 are by Ron Cox
Copyright © 2016
All Rights reserved

Book Design: Ginger Legato

Abiquiu Press gratefully acknowledges the Rising Moon Gallery in Abiquiu, NM
for their assistance and support.

Abiquiu Press
PO Box 1207
Abiquiu, New Mexico, 87510

First Edition
Printed in the United States of America
ISBN: 9780692809457

This collection is dedicated to Rob Dean

THAT OLD ELM

A vision of green fills my window
The topmost branches rise beyond the limits of the frame

Years ago I wanted to chop it down
"Chinese Elms are weeds" I insisted
You argued that only fools destroy trees in deserts
Where every tree is a sacred gift

Now your bones lie just outside the drip line
While my heart is rocked in waves of green
I come into my body
I become myself again

You were right

CONTENTS

WINTER

SPRING

SUMMER

FALL

Love, Death, and Flowing Water

WINTER

It is not an accident that the Western calendar begins just after the winter solstice when the days are darkest. The Eastern calendar begins about a month later when the days are coldest. The ancients knew that during those dark, cold days, when our lives are most limited and difficult, the year is beginning. The quality of winter lays the foundation for the harvest. Will there be enough snow? Will the freeze be deep enough to kill the bugs? The qualities we fear and resent are the qualities that support life in the days that follow. Equally, our times of suffering, loss, and grief lay the foundation for the fullness of our lives. In the face of death we find the stirring of life and meaning. In the depths of cold and dark we celebrate. We wish each other Happy New Year.

THE WARRIOR'S PATH

To tease beauty
From grief

To find grace
Amidst struggle

To hold compassion
For our fellows,
To escape lonely exile

To rest in the light of faith
When nights are dark

To fuse clarity and acceptance

To hold tight to gratitude

To continue step by step
Though we are lost

To retrieve all that we are
To bring love on the journey

To remain curious and committed
In our smallest acts

This is the warrior's path

RETURN OF THE EAGLE

As constant as the calendar
When the days turn cold and dark, she returns

As faithful as a lover
She sits in the snag across the river
While I watch her stillness
She does not move
She waits
She swoops
A flowing arc of purpose
The strike
A trout flashing in her talons

This is a gift
Of the cold, dark days

Sorrow becomes bliss

We float into ecstasy

Warm beds call us home

INSOMNIA

I lie awake as the first breath of a new day
Stretches toward dawn
My heart is full
My dead gather round me like lovers
Each bending to bestow a kiss
They have waited patiently for my call
While I was distracted in this luscious world
Busy doing and being

Alone in this darkness
I remember
I hear their sweet murmurs
I imagine their soft touch
I am woven into a net
That stretches beyond time
Beyond space
Beyond being
All the dimensions hold me
I do not wish to sleep

Light on the water
Ducks in the snow
The grasses stutter
Palsied by a bitter wind
My head sinks
My eyelids droop
As I sit near the wood stove
In the warmth of the fire
Before the miracle of double-glazed windows

Grace washes me clean
Ideas scatter like dry leaves
My heart relaxes

The price for the wisdom of age?
The dead are stacked around me like cordwood
They loved me once and love me still
But they are gone and I am here
Still loving them as I have always loved
In the flood of moments each with its own diversion
May they now receive what I did not give then
May they know that beyond what I offered
Lay what I would have given
Had I been different than I was
I offer my memories, reaching toward the receding shades
More faithful to my dead now than while they lived

I stand at the chasm's edge looking out
When I recede into the mystery
I will leave words unspoken
Acts not done
I will also leave memories of connection
For there are moments
When isolation shatters and we are one
This is our way
Remembering and forgetting
Finding that this poor loving is all we have
And everything we need

JOY

Fog slips down the face of the mesa
Transforming chamisa and creosote bush into ice-sheathed crystals
That glitter where the blanket is torn to admit the sun
The world is so quiet
Even the voice of the river is muted

LOSS

I speak not of the phoenix rising from the ashes
I speak of ash
Job lost
Lover gone
My child cold on his pillow
Not the loss which leads to gain
For that is the way of the world
I speak of the loss which overshadows gain
Of loneliness
Of fear of failure
Followed by failure itself
In that darkness you meet your faith

Faith which flourishes
Only in the light of triumph
Is not faith but a scheme
A contract signed with fingers crossed
Those who seek success are offered many tools
Those who seek the Divine are offered loss
The prize torn from our grasp
Strength and cunning come to nothing
The hard shell of knowing and doing shattered

Only there, where grief rests
Like sky, like stone
We meet ourselves as we are
Naked and washed in God's tears
Washed in God's tears and knowing
Those tears are the Source

Not for us, old age,
It was not to be our destiny
We were vibrant, creative, young
We rejected all limitations
We fractured thought with psychedelics
Shed our clothes, if not our inhibitions
Left our homes to stand on the side of the road
With thumbs outstretched
We avoided gluten and red meat
Our grains were whole
How is it we grew old?

Our knees ache
Our eyesight fades
Our memories retreat
Among our friends one or another has an illness that frightens
A lapse that causes us to wonder
Should something be done?

How could we have prepared for what was not to be?
Who can believe that body or mind will weaken?

When at last we came to know what we never believed
We found hidden inside the mystery of age a treasure
We had gained more than we could lose

As the container failed
It revealed its contents
Sweet and beautiful beyond all measure

WE HAVE GROWN OLD

We have grown old, my love
We held many, before we held each other
Lovers lost to us now
Through mishaps, missteps, mistakes

Some left in anger
Some in grief
Some slipped from our embrace
When the winds of time
Parted the veils of death

We are grown old, my love
Now we hold each other
And in each other
We hold sweetness

I come to the end
I don't recognize the place
I struggle on

WHEN THE DAYS CLOSE DOWN

When the days close down
The hours fill with necessity
Bring wood
Keep the fire burning
So the pipes don't freeze
Check the chickens
Make meals that are simple and hearty
Do not go about when the roads are icy

Tonight as I lay under two quilts
I plan to drive to the hot springs

Shattering the limits of necessity
Is such joy

SPRING

Spring. The word evokes hope, colored eggs, and blossoms. The reality is different. The wind blows endlessly and mercilessly. When we run into each other at the post office we report that the wind is making us crazy. The temperature swings wildly so that the fruit trees blossom and then freeze again and again, sometimes wiping out the whole year's harvest. Spring is the time of change. We long for change and beg for change. But its arrival is turbulent. We wonder if we can survive the upheaval. In northern New Mexico our most important spring ritual emphasizes the crucifixion of Jesus that preceded the resurrection. This is our way.

NIGHT

How sweet to allow my senses
To draw into the circle of light
Cast by the lamp beside my bed
The world becomes mystery
I likewise pause
The night inhales
As I gather myself
Without striving
I remember who I am

All the forms and ways of the day
Sunlight weaving patterns
Glint, glare, and shadow
Cacti
Brown grass
Tiny moments of green
Pressed against the earth
Wind in the chamisa
All the forms and ways of being
Lie hidden in the darkness

We will rise up again tomorrow
But tonight we rest

SPRING WIND

For how many years have I cursed you
Harbinger of change?
I long for green shoots and daffodils
Placid and contained
But feel instead your insistent slap
And the scent of your long journey
The clean sharp smell of lanolin and wood smoke
The sweet and painful reminder of orange blossoms and auto exhaust
The faint sting of salt water, the barest hint of ginger and bitter herb

To release my irritation
I borrow another man's memories
I am a boy lying on a roof
Wrapped in your power
My wild joy reaches into your answering embrace
I welcome the shifts that you foretell.
I know that change is the only constant

The invisible, through persistence
Scours rock

WINDS OF CHANGE

The winds of change are blowing
Fearful and exciting
The rivers of change are in flood
What will they wash away?
The surface remains smooth
If not untroubled
Over tea we wonder
What is coming?
What will remain?
Our health? Our knowledge?
Our children? Oh, our children
How can we hold them safe?
What of our wealth, our homes, our possessions?
What can we carry, safe, to the other side?
Nothing

We lie awake with fat bellies and full hearts
We try to cling to structures
Which offer safe haven
While facing the whirlwind
Which can set us free
The winds have chosen

FAMILY

Family. The word stirs the cyclone
Of hunger, grief, and longing
For what was not but may yet be
Past and future pouring into each other

We meant no harm and harmed so often
We wanted what we could not give
Giving all we had to offer
We dismissed what we were given
Believing that it had no value
Unable to value what was already ours

I remember going for a drive
Lying on the front seat
With my feet on my father's thigh
And my head on my mother's
A bridge between my parents
Loved and loving
All I needed to be and know

Today the magpies tussle
Driving off the milder birds
The river overflows its bed
Sunlight glistens on the rapids
Spring green bursts from stark winter branches
A wild chartreuse aura
Everywhere exuberance
But inside me a restless longing
Like a song half remembered

Neither coalescing nor fading
I search distance and dimension
For love that flows without fear
A return to a time when my being was the bridge

Reeds clutched in gnarled hands
Grace flowing from acceptance
Bent before the wind

ROCK

Rock only seems unchanging
Looming over us and framing the limits of our vision
We feel the dark fire of basalt flowing from bottomless fissures
The frozen freedom of tuff exhaled from cataclysm
Red sandstone built grain by grain in the great sea bed
Shot through with a crystalline script in an indecipherable alphabet

We feel rock's silent ceaseless power
Ages are as nothing
As years follow one on the other
We find ourselves bent toward rock's resolve
Drawn into the orbit of its design
Our natures shaped by the rock under and around us

Slowly, slowly over scores of generations
And in the numberless hours of a single life
Rock's purpose becomes our purpose
Its unwavering patience calms our frenzy
We follow its imperceptible journey
Rock's minerals build the bones
Which hold our oldest story

To learn its wisdom
We need only listen
Silent and accepting
Until we hear rock's voice
Feel the stern embrace
Rest on the back of our mother, Earth

TWISTING MY ANKLE WHILE CARRYING MY GRANDDAUGHTER

Less than a moment
A nano moment
No time at all
My ligaments stretch
Grow long
Contacting the ground yet suspended
The Golden Gate Bridge of ankles

Shocking pain
The Golden Gate of exploding ankles
I do not drop my granddaughter
I do not hurl myself to the ground
I bring my foot down slowly

It takes no thought
Nothing is more normal
Not love but survival
Ancestors unknown to me insist that I protect her
It is no choice
This choice made before I was born
A choice made by the Whole
For the Whole
For the future of the Whole

I put my foot down slowly
I walk

Delicious hunger
This flavor of desire
Too lovely to sate

MOTHER

I could fall into your arms forever
Dissolving into the infinity of your embrace
Your love is as hard as the heron's cry
And as fierce as the eagle rising from the river
I am not called to any other
You are my home and my journey
I rest my head on your shoulder
When you whisper, 'my daughter'
I become myself
You see me as I am
Yet you love me

RELATIONSHIP

From what well do we draw the courage
To risk again, to turn again
To tell each other
That we will try again
To care for each other
From what fountain
Can we drink the life-giving water?

From love itself

We hesitate to speak the word
For we are modern, injured people
We know that love can wound
And the pledge of love can wither
Yet we also know
That love can soothe the wounds it carves
And the world buds anew in spring

SUMMER

The joy, the soothing green, endless light, but always the possibility of drought and flood. Our lives are dependent on water yet the rains can fail. Summer is sustained by the gift of water, its beauty and its healing magic. Those of us who attempt to put down roots in this dry land are drawn to its mystery and power, but we know that we live here only with the permission of the rain. We also know this permission can be revoked. We walk among the ruins of villages from which the ancestors were driven by drought. We have neighbors whose homes have been swept by flood. We dance at the edge of the desert on the banks of its rivers. The dance is so sweet because it is not certain.

THE ACEQUIA PRAYS THE LAND TO LIFE

Carved into red earth
By hands now lost to history
A ribbon of life flows among the willows
Shimmering silver green
Filled with the scent of the river
It whispers of another world

LOVE, DEATH, AND FLOWING WATER

Love, death, and flowing water
There is nothing else
Catching, breaking free
Flowing on
Moment follows moment
The flowing arc of a day
Soaring over all the song of love
Weaving each moment to the other
The net which holds our souls

With your morning coffee
You search the threads of dream
That cling to your robe
And swallow the sweet bitterness
That pulls you forward into morning

In waking and in sleeping
In sweetness and in struggle
The lullaby of dying
Murmurs in our veins
This is not forever
We are not forever
Triumph and defeat
Gain and loss
All will be washed away

If this murmur does not set us free
Death itself will release us

TIME

It's always happening at once
Time, weightless as an origami bird
In my cereal bowl
Rice Krispies
The taste of breakfast in my childhood home
Became the hallmark of my mother's visits
My children skimmed cream in anticipation of her pleasure

The face that looks from the photo
Of me with my granddaughter
Is my mother's face
More surely than the one in the photo of my mother and my daughter
Which does not exist, or exists only in the land of my longing
For a time that was not, but could have been
Or may yet be, for it surely is
As my brother Jim, dead these thirty years
Stares from his namesake's face, my son
And what of my daughter who felt terror each time she skied
Is she my brother returned to us from the avalanche?

My own life overruns its banks toward the unseen.
The river of electricity and chemistry that I call myself
Future and past linking in one flow, drawing from each other
Singing in counterpoint the same song
The song of me, which is more than I could have imagined
Yet known by the stars at my birth
And known by myself at my death
This is the telling of the tale I have always known
Yet wait for someone else to begin the phrase
Hesitating while memories coalesce, the known and unknown
Filling the bowl of self
Overflowing into all that waits to flower

DROUGHT

Orange and fuchsia tear the evening sky
Another day closes without the blessing of rain
We murmur of a dry history
Repeat tales told by a father's father
Now laid in the red earth
We have not known drought until now
We share tales of villages drier than ours
Their ditches will not see water this year
What of their crops, and their wells?
We do not speak of our fears for ourselves
But we feel the dread circling
Just beyond our sight and instinct
In southern counties still distant
In the shadow of not here, not yet
The noose grows tighter
The red earth dries
Who can we petition?
How have we come to this helplessness?
We who have bent our knees to no one
Who have never waited on the Lord

Bouquets of minnows
Flashing beneath the surface
Just beyond my reach

THE HERON'S CRY

The sound of a madman wrestling a cat
A heron's cry pierces the darkness

Provoked by a skunk or raccoon
Does she dare to rise in the darkness

Flapping her heavy wings
Heading upriver to hide?

Or does she stand in the river
Safe and afraid?

FIERCE WATER

This summer is marked by angry rains
Storms that tear the land
Surge down the arroyos
Turn the rivers red
Lick at an unlucky home

Still we rejoice at the fierce water
How could we not?
Seeing the blush of green on the hillsides
Deep and cool where the llanos lay back
We will never curse water in this dry land

THE RIVER'S SONG

The voice of the river
Is like an old camp song
Like the call "Ollie, Ollie Ox In Free." on a summer evening
Like my mother's voice.
Nothing could be more normal and more poignant
I am the river's child
My pulse echoes her lullaby
Her memories flow through my fingers
Washing away delusion
Reminding my bones of their continual motion
Easing them into the healing
Which is the river's song

Bird strikes the window
Neck broken like bent willow
Some rules are not known

BADGER TRILOGY

June twenty-third
Baby roosters
Ounces of fluff and fury
Establish their hierarchy
Quarter-inch talons extended
As they hurl themselves
At miniature opponents
Cruelty and cunning
Victory and defeat
Beauty and foolishness
Nature does not judge

June twenty-ninth
Furry, clown face
Looks up at me
Black and white stripes across her eyes
Floppy paws
Fast as a shadow
I see the tracks that found
The weakness in the wire
She tunneled under
Feathers litter the yard
The tiny roosters helpless
Before the badger's claws
Nature does not judge

July sixteenth
A cry breaks the darkness
Then silence
Scanning the trees with my flashlight
I turn to see the black and white stripes

In the turkey house
Again feathers like fallen leaves
Again the poults slaughtered
A hen's red flank
Flesh opened with those great claws
A ten-foot tunnel under the coop
Dug with remarkable persistence
And certain cunning
Badger has become my enemy

SUMMER DAWN

Soft grey flows
From dark mystery
Forms emerge
Surfaces appear
Colors explode
All manner of beings manifest and are seen
They exist again
As they were
But rested and made new
In the magic of dawn

Love calls softly
Sensing rather than hearing
The sound of the self

The plover beckons
With her broken wing
She draws us away

GRANDMOTHER COTTONWOOD

Your silence holds wisdom
So calming that I am drawn into myself
For a green moment which spans eons
You exhale slowly

The wind stirs the cottonwood branches
Rocking my restless heart
I call to the river
Carry my dreams to the sea

I sleep in the song of the river
It wraps around me like Ganesha's soft trunk
Telling me that no harm can come in this world
Woven so carefully of love

MEMORY

Everywhere I see layers
Scenes visible only to my inner eye
People and places appear
As they were
All those years ago
Empty fields now subdivisions
Cheap apartments now luxury condos
My grandchildren's parents in diapers learning to walk
J W Owen in the double Quonset hut
The pride of Espanola
Where I bought a pot to piss in
My own history
Held in a million, million pictures
Curly bugs in the dirt outside my house
The fierce cold as my body breaks
The surface of a mountain lake

Beauty, love, and laughter delight again
Shock and grief are softened by distance and time
I see my son happily jumping in the back seat
As I drive down the mountain
After finding my brother's body
The picture is clear
But transformed by my bond with a soul
That is both my brother and not my brother
Being now freed from the limits of flesh

SWIMMING AT SUNSET

The lake unrolls before me
As I lie upon its shining surface
Alone in the silence
Which flows out toward the hills
And the setting sun
The lake is mine
As I am hers
Together and alone
In the vast peace
Of our kinship

FALL

There is a folk story which repeats in slightly different forms—the hero throws a great party at the height of which he suddenly dies. This plot is always shocking and creepy. However, in the cycle of the seasons we go to this party every year. It is always wonderful. We delight in the brilliant colors as the trees turn gold and red. Gardens pour out their bounty and we fill ourselves and our larders with wonderful foods. The skies are bright, the weather crisp. Then one morning we wake to the killing frost. The flowers and vegetables are dead in the garden, the plants that were green yesterday lie in brown piles. Death is all around us. Yet we do not mourn the loss. Our most playful rituals mark this transition: Halloween, Dia de los Muertos. We have known the cycle long and long. We celebrate.

GREY SKY ABOVE SILVER WATER

Grey sky above silver water
My jacket does not stop the cold
Flocks of seagulls rest on the ocean
By the railroad tracks
The screech of the wheels
More demanding than the screech of gulls

I was born to the high desert
My parents and my children are desert born
We are strangers to the sea
Yet the gentle rocking of the waves echoes the rhythm of my heart
My body remembers the salt smell on the wind

There is a lineage older than memory
Older than the tales told by a desert people
It rests in cells and in veins
Drawn by the call of grey and silver
I have come home to the sea

WEDDING PHOTOGRAPH

That picture must be somewhere
Taken on the eve of my wedding

What force propels us to
Fling our frail souls into the fire
From which we emerge transformed, if we emerge at all?

Transformed through our intimacy not simply with each other
But also with our demons
The shock of recognizing ourselves

FALL AFTERNOON

Trees wild in red, gold, and purple
A brilliant sun suspended in a sharp blue afternoon
White and grey clouds scatter across the face of the sky
The color, the tang, the sweetness
Yet our thoughts turn toward winter
We prepare
Harvest and store
Stack wood

This most beautiful of seasons
Feels like a bridge
Stretched between life and death
A moment of great exaltation
Invites the journey into darkness

TSIPING RUINS

The lure of the ancestors is quiet
But strong
Clay, stone, wood
Shaped by human hands
With attention and intention
To create a force so powerful
The air still ripples after seven hundred years
Can you hear the chatter of a thousand voices?
Can you see the earth and sky that held them?
The breeze that brushes your skin brushed theirs
Seven hundred years is nothing

Gently becoming
Languid evening light
A mantle of gold

Knitting the garment
Took so many lifetimes
I long to run naked

DARKNESS HAS BEEN MY REFUGE

Darkness has been my refuge
Soft release from the speed of day
I feel safe as I walk into the dark
Until I trip over a stone retaining wall

I plunge down
My face hurtling toward the earth
My legs arc behind me in the blackness
The bright dark rushes past my body
Where is the shock to stop this fear-filled dive?

My thoughts explode
They run forward and backward through time
Overlapping yet distinct
What injury waits?
Will I live to know?
Will time flow out from this endless fall
Or draw into itself to disappear?

At last the blessed ground
The pain is everywhere
The pain screams I am alive
I am here, alive on this earth

My torn face is soothed by the puddle of blood that cradles it
The body I used without thought can still move

I stand
I walk toward the light

UNDERGROUND AT MCALLISTER AND MARKET

I have come to the city
From a village
I stand before gleaming portals
To the underworld

The crowd breaks around me
Like a river
For I walk slowly
Reading each sign

Along the walls
The homeless wait like refugees
Seeking shelter and warmth
A woman with a sweet manner
Gets all my change
Then a young man sitting on the floor
Reminds me of my son
I promise to return

I stand in confusion
Before the ticket vending machines
Searching for instructions
Clues
Anything

A kind brown face
Wrapped in the uniform of homelessness
Comes out of the crowd
Layers of dirty clothing
Missing teeth
His short dreadlocks are a result

Not a statement
He is not racing toward a destination
He is here

Gently, he learns my destination
Presses the buttons
Tells me how and where to pay
I slip a five-dollar bill into the slot
We both know how much I need his help

I explain that I have made a promise
To the boy on the floor behind us
My mentor's smile brightens
He's my friend
He draws two quarters from his pocket
I take them to the youngster on the floor

A ticket silently slips from the steel wall
Quarters clang
I take the ticket
My mentor takes the change

The arc of the bough
Fills my heart. Beyond
What my mind can hold

How dare I attempt
A leap into the unknown?
How can I stay here?

LATE FALL NIGHT

The cicadas no longer click in the trees
The song tonight is sweet, high pitched, soaring
Have the cicadas been silenced by the cold
Relinquishing the night to crickets?
Or have they been transmuted by the nearness of the killing frost
Coming fully into their song just before they die?

LOVE POEM

How to write a love poem?
It must be simple
To slip into the day
Like scrambled eggs
It must be flexible
To bend with the time
Yet it must be strong
For we throw ourselves
Against its net with fury
It must be humble
It must be sweet
To lure us into vulnerability
Soothing, to ease the pain
That we cause each other
It must be as beautiful
As the light in my lover's eyes

Poetry of grief
Comes easily
Sharp and bitter longings
Flow freely
But the quiet happiness of love
Accepted and affectionate
The bread and butter of our days
How to catch that on the page?

The branch dripping light
We cannot compel the joy
Each drop has its moment

Your love is so clean
So ruthless, bright, and sweet
It scours the three worlds

I CLING TO BEAUTY

When I am knocked off balance
When my hopes are hijacked by my fears
When my thoughts become tangled
When I feel lonely
I cling to beauty
My guardian and anchor

Beauty is with me always and everywhere
In a line of hills
In the sunlight on a blackgreen feather
In a stranger's face
In the sweetness of your touch
When you reach out while sleeping
I do not know, and it does not matter,
If you know you are holding me

GRACE

We own nothing
Not even ourselves
Death is woven into all we love
All we hold dear rests in its shadow
Our possessions will outlive us
Then they too will crumble
All we have built will turn to dust

Those who experience this shock
For it is always shocking
Have been kissed by God's grace

God's grace
Harsh and brilliant under the sun
Fierce and deep beneath the stars
We can neither command it
Nor seduce it
It is whole unto itself
It offers us nothing other than what is

Immutable yet transformed

Bobble and paddle
Tumble, dip, and rise
Drift on the current

GRATITUDE

Thanks to the Abiquiu Poetry Group whose appreciation and support gave me courage. Many thanks to friends who read the manuscript and gave their time for editing.

In grateful acknowledgment of Ginger Legato and Abiquiu Press for bringing this book into the world.

Lastly, to my children and grandchildren. They are my joy.

ABOUT THE AUTHOR

Oro Lynn came to Abiquiu in the 1970's and never left. She settled by the Rio Chama where she built two homes, farmed, became a nurse, raised and buried children, was nourished by friendship. Having spent forty years on the river's banks she is now learning the lessons of age—that to grow old with grace and understanding requires unflinching honesty, generosity, and courage.